GOOD ENGLISH

JAMES M. TOLBERT

GOOD ENGLISH

COMMENCEMENT DAY ADDRESS AT ST. JOHN'S COLLEGE

MAY 1982

JAMES M. TOLBERT

BLACK BELT PRESS

Montgomery

Black Belt Press
105 S. Court Street
Montgomery, AL 36104

Cataloging-in-Publication Data
978-1-961938-21-2 (paperback)
978-1-961938-22-9 (ebook)

This essay was given as a commencement
speech at St. John's College in
Annapolis, Maryland, in 1982.

Printed in the United States of America

The illustration on the cover is an 1869 depiction by
Anonymous of the Library of the British Museum in London,
England, reproduced from the collection of The Rijksmuseum
in Amsterdam, The Netherlands.

BLACK BELT PRESS ∼ MONTGOMERY, ALABAMA

*The Black Belt, defined by its dark, rich soil, stretches across
central Alabama. It was the heart of the cotton belt. It
was and is a place of great beauty, of extreme wealth and
grinding poverty, of pain and joy. Here we take our stand,
listening to the past, looking to the future.*

CONTENTS

MAY 23, 1982

About that word *emeritus*. It's Latin, of course. Latin has a noun, *meritum*, meaning merit, worth, value, importance. It also has that little prefix *e-*, meaning out of, as in out of work, out of gas, out of luck. So emeritus means out of merit, out of worth, out of value, out of importance. St. John's President Emeritus Richard Weigle may argue that interpretation, and any Latin scholar will attack it. But I've distorted the facts only enough to make my point. Good seminar practice.

So you seniors have taken me out of emeritude and placed me here, to talk to you. Your request was a happy surprise, and I am more grateful, more deeply moved, than you can imagine and full of the affection that began with certain freshman tutorials about four years ago, which I suspect are not unconnected with your invitation. It is this affection, for the members of those tutorials and for all St. John's students (almost all), that has led me to choose the subject of my remarks today. You do so many good things so well that I cannot pass up this last opportunity to help you with one thing you do *not* do well.

My Subject is good English. I shall try to persuade you that you do not speak or write good English, and that good English is important, and to suggest some things you can do to improve your English.

St. John's has done well by you in many respects. You have completed the best undergraduate program in the world, with the help of the most dedicated faculty in the world. But you have had little or no help with your English. When could such help have been given? Seminars and tutorials would founder if a tutor interrupted with "Miss Jones, you have just mispronounced *spontaneity*" or "Mr. Smith, that last sentence of yours violated the principle of parallelism."

In paper conferences, it has seemed more important to your tutors to help you clarify your thinking than to help you punctuate your sentences properly. More *can* be done, however, I think. To say that the program is the best in the world is not to say that it cannot be better.

Let us consider, then, the state of student language. I shall mention only some of the things I observed repeatedly during twenty-six years here; you are still guilty of them, unless there has been an unpublicized revolution in the last three years. You are not alone. Almost the whole English-speaking world is guilty of the same offenses. At St. John's, however, where one lives intimately with the greatest books and discusses them constantly, and studies Greek and French with care, English should be more highly respected, and more competently used.

First of all, then, most of you often use bad grammar. I had occasion this year to read a brilliant paper by one of the brightest of St. John's students, and in it I found the words "concerning she." You say "between you and

I," "for my roommate and I, " as if the right word, *me*, were an obscenity. And the taboo on *me* has infected the objective forms of other personal pronouns, especially in pairs. I have found "to he and I" in the *Washington Post*. The opening words of a letter from the National Committee for an Effective Congress to its members found its way to *The New Yorker* magazine of May 17, under the heading "Letters We Never Finished Reading"; it began, "Dear Member, For you and I the 1982 elections . . ."

You think *phenomena, criteria,* and *media* are singular. You say "this phenomena" and "this criteria"and "the media is." But those words are plurals, and first two—shame on you—are Greek words.

You say, "I feel badly," which can mean only that your fingertips are numb. You say, "I sat my books on the table and laid down"; you might more correctly say, "I laid my books on the table and sat down." You are equally confused about *who* and *whom*, and about *shall* and *will.* (So was General MacArthur when he said, "I shall return." He meant "I will return," if he wanted to express determination.)

Your sentences begin with dangling modifiers:

> Walking to my seat, the curtain rose.
> When nineteen years old, my grandmother died.

You violate the principle of parallelism:

> He has written on Virgil, Dante, and is planning a paper on Milton.
> He described Virgil as imitative, Dante as divine, and the sublimity of Milton.

(This last sentence I have modeled on one spoken two weeks ago by Mr. Reagan's acting press secretary.)

LET US GO ON from grammar to the words you use. You choose bad words and misuse good words. Herbert Read begins his book *English Prose Style* with a chapter on words, and begins the chapter with this paragraph:

> Words are the units of composition, and the art of Prose must begin with a close attention to their quality. It may be said that most bad styles are to be traced to a neglect of this consideration; and certainly if style is reduced in the last analysis to a selective instinct, this instinct manifests itself most obviously in the use of words.

When I open my mind to the subject of the words you use, a flood of abominations pours in, and I can hardly still the flow long enough to take hold and begin. But begin I must.

George Orwell, author of *Animal Farm* and *1984*, wrote in 1946 an essay called "Politics and the English Language." In it he quotes a verse from Ecclesiastes;

> I returned and saw under the sun, that the race is not to the swift, nor the battle to the strong, neither yet bread to the wise, nor yet riches to men of understanding, nor yet favour to men of skill; but time and chance happeneth to them all.

Then Orwell translates the verse into what he calls "modern English":

> Objective consideration of contemporary phenomena compels the conclusion that success or failure in competitive activities exhibits no tendency to be commensurate with innate capacity, but that a considerable element of the unpredictable must invariably be taken into account.

The first of these two sentences is concrete; the second abstract. The first has forty-nine words but only sixty syllables; the second, thirty-eight words and ninety syllables. The first has four words of Latin origin, and they are everyday words like the rest: *returned, battle, favour,* and *chance*; the second has eighteen words of Latin origin and one of Greek. The first has six vivid images; the second, none. "Still," Orwell concludes,

> if you or I were told to write a few lines on the uncertainty of human fortunes, we should probably come much nearer to my

imaginary sentence than to the one from *Ecclesiastes*.

H. W. Fowler's *A Dictionary of Modern English Usage* is the great book on usage. Its author is called, by a recent writer on English, "the immortal Fowler" and "the Blessed Fowler." Fowler recognizes this prevailing tendency of modern English as a sickness, calls it "abstractitis," and says this:

> The effect of this disease, now endemic on both sides of the Atlantic, is to make the patient write sentences like ... *The availability of this material is diminishing* instead of *This material is getting scarcer*; *A cessation of dredging has taken place* instead of *Dredging has stopped*; *Was this the realization of an anticipated liability?* instead of *Did you expect you would have to do this?* And so on, with an abstract word always in command as the subject of the sentence. Persons and what they do, things and what is done to them, are put in the background, and we can only peer at them through a glass darkly. It may

no doubt be said that in these examples the meaning is clear enough; but the danger is that, once the disease gets a hold, it sets up a chain reaction. A writer uses abstract words because his thoughts are cloudy; the habit of using them clouds his thoughts still further; he may end by concealing his meaning not only from his readers but also from himself.

I now try to choke you with abstract words and develop in you such an allergy to the excessive use of them that you will break out in red welts if they begin to accumulate in your own writing. I give you a paragraph written by an editor of a review published by the U.N. Center for Regional Development, a review called "Asian Development Dialogue," which announces on a preliminary page that the magazine prefers articles "which are concise, clear and jargon-free." Here is the paragraph:

Our lead article views essential features of a framework for a comprehensive regional development analysis, plan formulation and implementation process which UNCRD has developed in connexion with training cum regional development planning study exercises in Indonesia, Pakistan, and the Philippines. Comprehensive in this sense refers to coordination and integration of development efforts (broadly defined) for a particular geographic space. Concern with development of a specific sub-national area does not imply that analysis and planning can be restricted simply to that politico-administrative level. Pertinent national and micro-level views and requirements need to be considered as well, and this suggests that multi-level approaches be pursued. An additional consideration is the "critical minimum information" for comprehensive regional planning and development whose operationalization requires the not-insig-nificant task of determining information precedence relationships—or principal types of decisions and associated infor-mation flow—in the process of analysis, planning and implementation. However, attainment of comprehensive planning and development in actual practice is more often influenced by certain characteristics of existing planning procedures and institutional arrangements than it is by availability of techniques. In other words,· issues of polity and society are not easily divorced from technical and administrative aspects of development analysis and planning.

An allied affliction, which may be called sesquipedaliphilia, is the love of long words. And you know *you* love them, in your own writing, and are proud of them, and are awed by an august assemblage of long words in the writing of others. But good English consists mainly of short words. And most short words come from Anglo-Saxon, long words from Latin or Greek. Fowler again:

"The better the writer, the shorter his words" would be a statement needing many exceptions for individual persons and particular subjects; but for all that, it would be broadly true . . . Those who run to long words are mainly the unskilled and taste-less; they confuse pomposity with dignity, . . . and bulk with force . . . There are often reasons why shortness is not possible; much less often there are occasions when length, not shortness, is desirable. But it is a gen-eral truth that the short words are not only handier to use, but more powerful in effect; extra syllables reduce, not increase, vigour.

I open *Paradise Lost* and *The Idylls of the King*, and at each first opening there face me:

Know ye not, then said Satan, fill'd with scorn / Know ye not mee? ye knew me once no mate / For you, there sitting where ye durst not soare.

And in those days she made a little song / And called her song "The Song of Love and Death," / And sang it; sweetly could she make and sing.

Fifty-six words, of which fifty-two are monosyllables. Slightly selected passages, indeed, but such as occur on nearly every page; and these are not exercises in one-syllable words for teaching children to read; they are the natural as well as the best ways

> of saying what was to be said. . . . What is
> here deprecated is the tendency among the
> ignorant to choose, because it is· a polysyl-
> lable, the word that gives their meaning no
> better or even worse.

Perhaps the superiority of the short word will emerge clearly from the following pairs:

diurnal	daily	deracinate	uproot
terminate	end	relinquish	let go
countenance	face	capitulate	give up
obtain	get	endeavor	try
utilize	use	eradicate	wipe out

IN THE THIRD PLACE, your language is full of *unnecessary* words, and these words obscure your meaning. The point that must be made here is that unnecessary words are not merely unnecessary but harmful. Every word counts, for good or ill. Alexander Pope says, *Words are like leaves; and where they most abound / Much fruit of sense beneath is rarely found.*

With your abundant superfluity you assert your solidarity with most of the rest of the English-speaking world. In newspapers, on television, in all places where politicians and other public figures gather, in letters personal and impersonal, indeed in nearly all sustained oral and written expression, including private conversation, unnecessary words sow confusion, bury meaning, choke communication. A student says to me, "In my opinion, I think he's, you know, a very strong-type individual," meaning "I think not strong."

The airline stewardess says, "Ladies and gentlemen, at the present time we would like to ask you to please make sure your seatbelts are securely fastened," meaning "Fasten your seatbelts." The sports announcer says, "That's Maryland's third punt in this particular football game," the last five words adding nothing, and therefore subtracting. The senator says, "I wish to inform the senator from Illinois that the answer to his question is in the negative," meaning "No." The too-careful scholar writes, "In my judgment it may not be an unjustifiable assumption that," meaning "I think that."

Using too many words is probably your besetting sin, as speakers and writers. The superfluity is all-pervasive with you. And I think is it usually due to lazy thinking, to carelessness. I wish I could remember who it was that wrote, "Please forgive this long letter; I haven't had time to be brief." I do remember that it was Anatole France who wrote to a young man that had exulted in his ability to write torrents fluently, "I hope to teach you to write with difficulty what you now write with ease." To write without using too many words is hard, but everybody can make a start. Here are some popular expressions that can, and therefore should, be reduced to a single word, or simply deleted:

a long period of time | a long time

I would appreciate it if you would | please

in the event that | if

it is interesting to note that | Delete

at the present time | Delete (now)

    From Strunk and White:

there is no doubt but that | doubtless (no doubt)

he is a man who | he

the fact that | Delete

The reader or listener does not know in advance which words to cancel or tune out. He has to sift through the whole, make quick judgments on subtle matters, throw out the mush, and assemble and make sense of the words that carry meaning. The more numerous the empty words, the less likely he is to get at your meaning, or at least the harder he has to work at the job. You owe it to your reader to avoid distracting him or making him slow his normal speed.

I have said that using too many words is usually due to carelessness. I come now to a habit of yours that is due to too much care, misdirected care, wasted care. You are persuaded that once you have written an important word, you must not repeat it within two inches, or two feet. You picked up that taboo at about the same time you were picking up the equally false notions that you must not begin a sentence with *and* or *but*, or end a sentence with a preposition, or split an infinitive. So you produce what Fowler calls, ironically, "elegant variation": You write, say, the word *football*—an unlikely hypothesis, but if you did write the word *football*, you would feel honor-bound then to write *spheroid, pigskin, oval, flying leather,* and maybe *laced ellipsis* before repeating *football.* I take the example from the sports page because sports writers are the champions of elegant variation—they and the radio and television sports announcers— probably because the happenings they report are the same day after day, and life without variety is murderous. Elegant variation is bad because when the reader finds *women* in one line and *ladies* in the next, he wonders what distinction is intended, looks for a clue, finds that the change has no significance, is irritated, and has to start over. Fowler seeks "to nauseate by accumulation of instances" drawn from official reports; I hope to nauseate you with part of a *Washington Post* sports-page article reporting the results of college basketball games. Here it goes, with the winning and losing teams called A and B, respectively:

> A trounced B
> A upset B
> A trimmed B
> A defeated B
> A nipped B
> A turned back B
> A outscored B

A hammered B
A whipped B
A stopped B
A routed B
A bested B
A tripped B
A stunned B
A beat B
A downed B

That should make you proof against the habit for life.

YOUR LINGUISTIC OFFENSES INCLUDE many words and phases that should not be used at all or that have other meanings than you think. Here personal taste and prejudice operate freely, and many persons in the audience will disagree with some of my judgments. But I shall pronounce them without qualification, as if no other judgment were possible.

It is bad taste to say—

Hopefully, the worst is over.

Hopefully, I shall finish the essay on time.

Hopefully, it won't rain.

Disinterested does not mean "without

interest. "It means "impartial," "without personal bias." A judge should be disinterested, but he should not be uninterested.

The word *individual* is not equivalent to *person*. Fowler calls this misuse "an uncouthness." Use *individual* only to contrast a person with society or some group of persons.

Nauseous means "causing nausea, sickening," or, by figurative extension, "intellectually repulsive." He who has the stomach disturbance is nauseated. When you complain, "I'm nauseous," the listener may think, "You are indeed."

That great and good man John Kieffer, who served St. John's as dean and interim president and for forty-six years as tutor, once said to me that all he had retained from his Harvard freshman English course was an aversion to *basic* and *basically*. I have long shared that aversion, I think only after hearing *basically* as the opening bomb of a lot of bombastic sentences. When so used it is quite empty; it is a cover for mental foot-shuffling, like the British "Well, actually," to kill time while the speaker gets himself in hand.

The expression *and/or,* with a diagonal mark between *and* and *or,* should not appear in your writing. Fowler calls it an "ugly device." Leave it to diagrams and tables and legal jargon. Instead of "a and/or b" write "a or b or both."

Say *"Fewer students* (not Less students) *attended this lecture than the preceding one."* Say *"The burglar left a large number* (not a large amount) *of fingerprints." Fewer* and *number* with plurals, *less* and *amount* with singulars—*"less money," "a small amount of sugar."*

There are many more such horrors. I'll glance at five of them: (1) Avoid *in depth,* with or without the hyphen. Say *thorough, careful, in detail.* (2) Leave *overall* to the working-man and say *total* or *in all.* (3) There is no such word as *irregardless.* (4) There is no such word as *alright. All right* is two words. (5) Stop adding the pseudo-suffix *-wise* to nouns: *He did all right marriage-wise. The city government has failed garbage-collection-wise.* In the early years of the rampant misuse of *-wise,* a cartoon in *Punch* showed an owl family in its tree: Father and Mother Owl and their son. Father Owl says to Mother Owl, "That's all very fine, but how's he getting along wise-wise?"

IN REMINDING YOU OF some of your deficiencies, I hope I have given you reason to believe that good English is important, but I want to make *sure* you believe it. (By the way, I am not going into your misspellings and mispronunciations. That way lies madness—and a long afternoon.)

In the first place, I believe that you don't know what you think until you have put it on paper. Talking helps, especially in a seminar or any other context where you are subject to criticism and try to be careful. But in talking you have many resources you don't have when writing—facial expressions, arm and hand gestures, rise and fall of voice, smiles and laughter, the telling pause. Such things help you persuade without clarifying your thought. Seminar conversation, and good conversation, is at best suggestive; it can surprise with sudden illumination; it can open the door to golden corridors. But it is only in writing that you can follow a corridor to its end. And the corridor becomes the long and bumpy road of shaping your idea in precisely phrased and tightly constructed sentences that build coherent and unified paragraphs that march in orderly inevitability from beginning through middle to end. Then you look at what you've written and you find that your idea isn't what you thought it was when you began. It is important to know what you think.

It's a truism that people are judged by the words they speak. Many of *you*, perhaps *most* of you, will have jobs requiring more *writing* than the average person—reports, speeches, letters, lectures, scholarly articles, legal briefs, and so on—and you will be judged by the words you *write*. At this point you may be saying to yourself, "I'll have a secretary who will turn my dictated muddle into good English." Where is that angel-secretary to come from? What institution of higher, lower, or middle learning is producing such paragons? Your secretary, if you are lucky, will hand you just what you dictated, in blocks of type that assert unapproachable authority and say, "Touch me if you dare." No, you will be on your own. You alone will write those words, sentences, paragraphs that others will examine and ponder and judge you on.

But the public good too, not your private good alone, will be affected by the way you speak and write. George Orwell says,

> One ought to recognize that the present political chaos is connected with the decay of language, and that one can probably bring about some improvement by starting at the verbal end.

"The decay of language" has been deplored in all times, and thoughtful persons have in all times found politics to be in chaos: But surely Orwell is right in believing that thought and language can corrupt each other and that shoddy thought and shoddy language are connected, probably causally, with shoddy politics. During the Watergate investigation, one of the President's men spoke of "the *enormity* of dealing with the President. " He meant, one supposes, the enormous responsibility and power of "dealing with the President." He didn't know that *enormity* means "excessive wickedness; outrageousness . . . A monstrous offense or evil." Throughout the Watergate hearings the President's men showed an ignorance of the precise meanings of words, constantly reminding me of Humpty-Dumpty in *Alice Through the Looking-Glass*:

> Humpty-Dumpty said, "There's glory for you."
>
> "I don't know what you mean by 'glory,'" Alice said.
>
> Humpty-Dumpty smiled contemptuously. "Of course you don't till I tell you. I meant, 'There's a nice knock-down argument for you!"
>
> "But 'glory' doesn't mean ' a nice knock-down argument,'" Alice objected.
>
> "When I use a word," Humpty-Dumpty said in rather a scornful tone, "it means just what I choose it to mean, neither more nor, less."

Much worse was the sleaziness of the Oval Office conversations revealed by the famous tapes, and I am thinking not of the expletives that were to be deleted but of the bad grammar, the meaningless abstractions, the cliches, the wordiness, the wrenching of nouns into makeshift verbs ("I am no-commenting on the whole business," said the Attorney General). The high linguistic crimes committed continuously in Washington reached a peak when political morality reached its lowest point.

The principal horror, however, is not what individuals say and write, no matter how highly placed, but the great mass of shoddy language, much of it anonymous, generated by Washington and every other center of political power and by nearly every television channel and newspaper. As the superfluous and meaningless and misleading words settle over the facts like snow, they blur the outlines and cover up the details, in Orwell's phrase.

Can one person make a difference? Can eighty-five St. John's graduates make a difference? I believe that every precisely used word makes a difference, every well-turned phrase, every well-built sentence, every tightly constructed argument makes a difference. If you speak and write well, you will at least not add to the din. What is more important, you will help establish high standards of language by which people can judge and condemn the bad language and escape its ill effects. I do not think the battle is lost. But it has to be fought every day.

After twenty-two years, more or less, of using bad English, you will have to work hard to learn to speak and write well. You must study some books about English, and you must practice. Most of the books you need I have mentioned. You probably have Strunk and White's *Elements of Style*. Its thinness—it has only seventy pages—may have given you false encouragement, but it does succeed in saying a lot of important things. Fowler's *Modern English Usage* (the second edition) is indispensable. Read it by the hour, learn to use it, keep it at your elbow. Since it was written for the British public, now and then it needs to be balanced by Wilson Follett's *Modern American Usage*, which also supplies some gaps in Fowler. A book I have found constantly helpful is *The Careful*

Writer, subtitled *A Modern Guide to English Usage*, by Theodore Bernstein, who was for years an editor of the *New York Times*. These four—Strunk and White, Fowler, Follett, and Bernstein—are books of reference. There are hundreds of books of rhetoric, many of them intended as textbooks, many of them to be read continuously rather than for reference. Two of these, not textbooks, are Robert Graves's *The Reader Over Your Shoulder* and Herbert Read's *English Prose Styles*; either is a good place for you to begin. Graves's book is of value for its emphasis on a writer's obligations to his reader, especially the obligation to be clear. Read's *English Prose Style* is a classic of its kind. It is elegant and eloquent, and it owes much to Aristotle and Fowler. Among the rhetorics intended as textbooks, I can recommend several that I have taught:

- Porter Perrin, *Writer's Guide and Index to English*
- James McCrimmon, *Writing with Purpose*
- Brooks and Warren, two books: *The Fundamentals of Good Writing* and *Modern Rhetoric*

But you must write in order to learn to write. Write as much as you can. Writers used to keep a "commonplace book, " a sort of personal journal in which they wrote comments short and long on anything and everything, copied striking passages from their reading, recorded memorable events, and so on. Try it. Write enough to get into the habit of writing. If possible, get some qualified person to read and criticize your writing. You are so intelligent. With much writing and much study of writing, you can learn to write better, and your speech will get better and better as a consequence.

Godspeed, and good speaking.

About the Author

St. John's College tutor emeritus James M. Tolbert was a native of Columbus, Georgia, who held undergraduate and master's degrees from Emory University and a doctorate in English from the University of Texas. During World War II, he served in counterintelligence in the Philippines and afterwards in Japan, and also in security at the Manhattan Project in Los Alamos, New Mexico. He taught at and chaired the English Department in Florence, Alabama, at what is now the University of North Alabama before joining the St. John's faculty in Annapolis, Maryland, in 1953. He was initially both a tutor and director of admissions before becoming a full-time tutor from 1972 until his retirement in 1979; he died in 1993. He was a beloved and esteemed figure on campus, a courtly and gentle Southerner who shepherded a generation of students into St. John's.

A Few Words about St. John's College

St. John's College in Annapolis, Maryland, is among the most revered institutions of higher education in the United States and was supported by, among others, Thomas Jefferson and James Madison. Nonsectarian from the start, the college began as King William's School in 1696 and was chartered as St. John's in 1784, making it the nation's third oldest college.

St. John's is a nationally recognized model for liberal education in large part due to a unique curriculum centered around the Great Books Program introduced in 1937 by educational reformers Scott Buchanan and Stringfellow Barr.

Their radical unified approach was and is based on the classics of Western thought and literature. Faculty members—called tutors, not professors—conduct seminars, tutorials, and labs through dialogue with small groups of students.

The curriculum spans literature, philosophy, theology, mathematics, science, music, and political theory built around "core readings" of the works of authors such as Homer, Plato, Aristotle, Euclid, Galileo, Newton, Shakespeare, Nietzsche, and Einstein. The teaching seeks to instill formal logic and critical reasoning. Greek and French are taught, there are no majors or electives, and all students follow the same course of study and submit a senior thesis.

St. John's attracts highly motivated students from across the United States and abroad. Enrollees are typically intellectually curious young men and women drawn to the college's discussion-based model, rigorous reading list, and philosophical approach to learning rather than vocational training.

A second campus opened in 1964 in Santa Fe, New Mexico, and shares the original structure and curriculum. Total enrollment across the two campuses is less than 1,000.

Notable alumni include Francis Scott Key, Ahmet Ertegun, Ben Sasse, and Douglas Hofstadter. Past presidents include John

McDowell, Stringfellow Barr, Richard Weigle, Christopher B. Nelson, and Nora Demleitner (2022–present). Significant tutors have included mathematician Jacob Klein, classicist Eva Brann, Plato scholar Seth Benardete, and biblical translator Robert Sacks.

St. John's College is an exemplar of "classical liberal education in the modern world. Its dedication to dialogue, reasoned inquiry, and the foundational texts of Western civilization makes it unique among American colleges. With a legacy reaching back three centuries and a curriculum that has changed little in nearly a century, it continues to attract students and educators passionate about the life of the mind."